bliNk

bliNk

Cameron Lowe

PUNCHER & WATTMANN

© Cameron Lowe 2025

This book is copyright. Apart from any fair dealing for the purposes of study and research, criticism, review or as otherwise permitted under the Copyright Act, no part may be reproduced by any process without written permission. Inquiries should be made to the publisher.

First published in 2025
Published by Puncher & Wattmann
PO Box 279
Waratah NSW 2298

info@puncherandwattmann.com

NATIONAL
LIBRARY
OF AUSTRALIA

A catologue record for this book is available from The National Library of Australia.

ISBN   9781923099548

Cover design by David Musgrave and Cameron Lowe

Printed by Lightning Source International

In memory of Norma Dorothy Hendy
&
Katie (Kit) Lowe

~

&
for Ada

>   to make
>
>   is to risk
>
>   making
>
>   a botch

—Harry Gilonis, *Rough Breathing* (2018)

Late-morning Western reverie as raindrops
turn rivulets trickling visions of
trickle-down economics
on the pane

Thought it was Josey Wales who said *it*
in *The Outlaw Josey Wales*
but he didn't—

Wales said: 'To hell with them fellas. Buzzards
gotta eat same as worms.' He said:
'Dying ain't much of
a livin, boy'—

It was John Vernon, said: 'Don't piss
down my back & tell me
it's raining'—

Antony & the percentages

wild night &
aren't we coming yet
to some fleshy pronouncement vis-à-vis
politics & Eros, blink & spit
dinky-di popular moonlight treacle
drizzled over wheat & mortgage belts?
I disclose here my 'thank your rabbit for the mothers'
homespun crouton sophistry &
any minute now another talking head
will start spanking out
the numbers

Grape days

1

Sound of shovels scraping
gravel, voices

of men—night's
heat

clinging still—

Awake to this, or
swimming

yet in sleep
you mumble—

A fly

is walking
on your forehead

2

    'Ten thousand women
        and I
            the only one
                in boots'—

        Today, a thousand
            cyclists
                all clad
                    in Lycra—

            Sirens of fire-trucks
                36° at 12
                    no figure 5
                        in gold—

3

Salmon in the cat's bowl,
chilli flower—

        I water
cyclamen, you display
new shoes.

The stopped
clock:

12:16

wind change—

Of the snow dome
you write:

'this is not a place
not a world…'

& yet—

4

After the heat, violence
       of wind, the sound of it

in trees—

sun on spider's web
       by the white chair

star pattern in chalk
on balcony
concrete—

details arranged, leaves
blowing down
the street

5

'Breathe it out quietly'
you write

'air thick as milk'—
The moon rises

over pines
police lights

on the esplanade—
You write:

'blackened leaves
swimming'—

Night presses in
leads nowhere—

scent of coriander
cinnamon

slow-cooking—

Summer fancy for idle limes

Thought, rest sweetly
in the shallows
of night

like a floating
thong, while the eye
falls asleep

& the ear, well
the ear gets busy
on a bender!

One-way conversation with Agapanthus

Trouble is
the reflective lyric pose
won't hold, when every time I greet you
vision splits (courtesy
Dr J's story concerning patient X's curious habit
of sticking random
objects—
    recall Dr's pause...
                  gesture...stalk
        &
    flower—up his...SURGICAL REMOVAL
REQUIRED...) It's true—
we're amazing strange, don't you think
Agapanthus.

Art Deco

After the rain, wander the arc
of the boardwalk

water kissing bars
of the shark-proof fence.

For Kent MacCarter

Let's face it Boss, we wear our luck outside
our pants, yet still—it seems—
one stinking truck
        of shite follows another
  then your
      Splendid News!
hits town
  Smile—
     salute—
          Oh yes, here's another stinking truck
            Sky fish are so hypnotic
              'Clippity clop clippity clop'
     A toast—
        'The towel's not thrown just yet'

Ascent

When I was a child, I met the best footballer of all time in the local sports shop. I thought him the best—my grandmother said it was true. She kept a portrait-magnet of him on her fridge. My father, who was with me, said: 'I thought he was bigger.' He looked huge to me; his neck bulged enormously from his white T-shirt. He smiled when he shook my hand.

A decade and a half later, I met him again, at the local pub. A lot had changed. He was still in the news, but not for football. His grey suit sat oddly on his shoulders. He was shorter than I was. I think he was drunk. I was drunk. He was still the best footballer of all time. I couldn't stop looking at him. He offered me a slice of cold pizza.

Leaving the Corio station

    he says /

        I said to them

    LISTEN—

        Let me tell you about this face—

    I paid a lot of money
for this face—

        This face is perfect

Everyday

—for Autumn Royal

stuck deep
    in ruts
        of minor chronicles
hiccups
    dog's breakfast
        lunch dinner
pedant's tongue—
        How sing it straight
    in all this fiddle?
Muck to eye to sore
seeing *is* as *if*
    holes punched
        in air the quick pulse
            step pulse leap crawling
        out of spillage
        chin up
        chin down every day
        rain hail brine
            you name it

Blush

1

The sudden blush on us you move
as wind sweeps across blue water
you move   the clouds

slide by   will not hold
thought or the thought
of—

to be inside   your motion
blush   on blush
in the sliding clouds

thought will not hold
the wind across blue water

2

Beside you then, sleepy head
sleepy hair, I brush—

each breath stirs
the whiteness

of white walls—
so the day

the day
rolls on—

sleepy hair, I brush—
the white sheet

each breath, you & I
sleepy head—

Sunday radio

Lichen patterns slate
black cat traces

gutters, thin wedge
of sun on dahlia

'que Dalila lia'
wrote Jacob

(different
impulse

an extra
dahlia)

car horn
water-skiers

Nina Simone
sings 'Stars'

January pastoral

Twitter, twitter, little
like gone all jelly soft in summer
light banana lounge sunscreen bikini-
    top
   'Does either Mr Bedient or Mr Hughes
     or myself know how
        a hangman thinks?' Is it green bin night
   or yellow?
      Cockatoo!
Alice Irene,
    no thirteen billion pillars of ash
   berries will ever wash dementia clean—nor
    the old songs cohere
      over the heads of the swimmers.

Bellegarde-du-Razès

I smoked
        on the terrace
in the twilight—
        only to find I prefer
the balcony
        in Geelong

Searching for Australians in the *LRB* bookshop

—for Laurie Duggan

Strange
      who you greet
on those shelves—
            who you don't.
I bought
      Harwood's
The Orchid Boat
          & headed south.

Two poems

1 Fuse

It's not often she wears jeans.
Full moon's stillness
to the east, spread of
dark branches.

    Slow graze
blue denim, the glass
vase with violet
orchids—
          yes
I objectify—

the rare fish
bone

    Foals Bread
marks the spine

2 Glow

'Now reach across the dark'
—Roy Fisher

There is a certain way of talking
about light globes.

    I will write
a big poem some day.

    Reflection
encounters reflection:
the window, dusk
bats flying out of
the mirror.

    The desire
to make it more
than it is.

There are prizes
for this—

White sauce

A stormy romance ends in the arms
of another, ends with 'too long at the bar'.
Am I marrying for money?
Should I hire a wig? I buy a book
on ways to disappear.
She licks the stranger's face.
I raise two flutes at the camera.
Snap, snap. You pretend indifference,
study the table of gifts.
'Stand and deliver or lie down
like a pig'. I love your shoulders,
but detest the cake.
Why is Vladimir attending the priest?
Who is that priest? You say:
'I've just popped in from Alaska'
& slip the ring from your finger.
It gets hot waltzing & I'm the one
wearing the white gown.

Tommy Dysart reads *A whistled bit of bop*

Is Ken. Is good.

Pastoral /
    'Asset management'

                      winter once more   & still
              the grapevine's crimson
                  leaves veil
              the front fence
                  as the number-cruncher
          declares
    'you should cut that back—
        it's a classic
      white picket
you've got there'

Nocturne

The carpet could be cleaner—
so could the world.
There's too much cayenne
in the soup.
The grand abstraction
is one approach
to the poem, I guess—
so too the eye
of the flea.
I can't even taste
the vegetables.
And love?
Mosquitoes are circling
the light globe—
Norma, dead now
a month.
After we cast the lilies,
Anne said: 'there's
room enough in there
for all of us'—

Ribbons

Little is known about workplace health promotion for bus drivers. That's how it started: a string of words shaping space into something resembling an idea. Of course, she said, there are always substitutes for the real thing. They worried at it, let it go, and in the rear view mirror there were the back slappers, as usual, jerking off over line breaks. You could say—as fact—dolphin were leaping through winter trees. You could say *this* is Australia, if you want it. Turning right, turning left, flicking radio stations, tapping out the hours. You could say here's a thing left behind a long time ago, the child's dream tilting in the sun. Stepping out, stepping in. If you listen long enough, they'll whisper to you: here's the key, *kid*; you're sure to find that special thing you've desired all along.

Friesland Farm under red clouds

Curiously
it was

ships
on fire

I saw
the

night
I turned

it upside
down

Correspondence

—after Lee Harwood

The night opens   stays open   a letter
marked *Par avion*   no brooch

for the artful   no lake
reflecting the woods—

    Only leaves   rain-slick
in streetlight   winter's postcard

plain enough   to say   *yes*
'brushing through'

Commission

—for Tamryn Bennett

Tired my eyes
    having done nothing
but speak
    turtle talk to tortoise
        cat—

  There is no
        beautiful magnolia
    poem to send—

  The petals are
      their own news—

        Go try painting the wind

Suspension

1

'The practical linoleum is tiresome, I propose
a peach-pink stone-fruit glaze (quarter-inch
with cedar skirts)' &
when the screaming lorikeets of spring go
wheresoever they do post the sun's demise
a single candle invites the hour
of soluble kiss.

2

'All I said was I wish I'd known
these parachutes, my love, were defective—
to plunge is exquisite caress, but there's mould
on the bathroom ceiling'. Rewind.
Now practice the art
of treading air.

Suburban incidental

—for Alan Loney

Morning sun casts shadow pickets—
    turtledoves bonking
on the barbeque

The tulips

Now they are spent
recall those petals

as faces, or
faces of clocks

or parasols
parting under

faces of clocks—
dress them

as painted hours
for seasons of

absent touch—
or any other

fancy you desire
to sell

"Duncan, hoist the spanker…"

—for DH

Oyster, oyster, on
the wall
   DAWNS
      A BIG DOG
         WOG (in crayon
  scrawled)—So it's written, so it's
read—'I need a keyboard
    to create'—
     Onions, mushrooms
    chard & bacon
   sautéed fetta, chilli flakes (*canso
     vida*, shanty fever)—

     Abandon captain, little ship
       the local pose is wearing thin.

The beginning

There is an envelope on a table by a window with a view of blue water. A plain white envelope, addressed to someone, the handwriting unclear even in the window's light. No stamp, just a name and address in black ink. It is a simple table of dark timber, oval shaped, yet otherwise unremarkable. The water is calm, a sea somewhere. No shore, just water and the darker line of horizon. So far there is only silence, the envelope in the light and the blue water. When the sound begins it seems to come from the envelope, it seems to hang in the light. Then it seems to come from under the table, and then from somewhere else in the room. There is the blue water beyond the window and the light on the envelope and the sound that is sharper now—sharper and…yes, it is clear what it is. Sharp in the light the sound, and the envelope on the timber table, and the blue water beyond the pane—when the door opens, the dark line of the horizon is there, stretching, stretching.

Chute

—for Corey Wakeling

Ready, please, Mr Music—
        The man desires music!
Old rotting boot abide
   a dribbly piss behind the shearing shed
the pines are falling down…
    Falling down—
        There's blood in the dag—
          There's—
            'Mr Curtsy…Mr Curtsy…
Mr Curtsy…'
      Mr Ned? Dead?
Cocky peeled the almond…
     'Dad! Dad!'—Cocky peeled the almond…
       There's blood in the fleece—
           There's blood on the—
                There's blood—

Rim

'One imagines himself/addressing his peers/I suppose.'
—George Oppen

Slid the candle a hand's-width
left along the table &
studied
the twist of flame in glass
& the lights beyond.

Ride

—for Kris Hemensley

Thought of the line
                the stops & starts
to the city—
         Blackburn's riff
on stations
     his 'Coney Island of the mind
to the Coney
Island of the flesh'
         a signal flicker
for signal fault
     right here
right now
   in Lara town, the song, the singing's
belated pulse—scoria   thistle
     You Yangs   *Day's eye*
Hold tight—

Time's shit sandwiches hurrying beer

Since hiccups are all that's left of the singing
        try sharper pencils
on your face—
    Try 'Chomei at Toyama'—
'That's a high-pressured hydraulic cleaning apparatus!'
      This, friend's a spinning mirror
                vision's borrowed plumes
        in ocean hues—
      Years of words refuse to wash—
        Where's baby?
'Doesn't a storm sky
              grow wonderfully enormous
     when you're not looking?' *Say it—no ideas*
                      got no clues—
'Just follow the yellow brick road…
                Follow the yellow brick road!'

Monuments / l o o k i n g o u t
    'the shitty little dogs on the corner'

      or spaces, edges
where cats roll

    out of night's
corrugations

      brittle divisions, wires

        the water
           wind-driven
                clouds streaming east

Hamptons lounge

—for Ken Bolton

I recline on it
to consider my
Rothkos!

Suns

the cat scratches
a page

of Eigner
circa 57

trace the marks
the presence

of now to
what was

surfaces
fresh ruts

in 'the old rutted
ground'

Soloist intimations

Surface to dare, clap & wave
idly as blowfly lands on beer can's lip
    plastic Buddha cracks
his Borgnine grin
        & Manager man sayeth: 'Consider Sun Tzu…
Sisyphus, the drying wings
of cormorant…
    Imagine riding the elephant'—
Heaving spring heatwave
red poetical jellyfish
      rash, sweaty stinky armpit thunder—
            'But the farmers had moved away,
            the barn was abandoned and the granary
            stood empty. And since winter was not far off,
            the little mice began to gather corn and nuts
            and wheat and straw. They all worked day and night.
            All—except Frederick.'

      *

    'No beetroot, please…'

      *

Meld song's mire balcony daze sun-bright Tuesday
hangover. Drop saw nail gun currawong map
of Croatia—
    Busted thong. Leafy street daydream
smiley life palaver. A job is a job
is a job. 'Are you
for real?'

*

'Yeah…nah…maybe'—
    'What is the scope of your work?' Huh?
'Scope.' Recall Dinger Bell: 'Ya got shit
in yr ears?' Add eyes. DOOR
THAT SLIDES.
Dear Sir.

Promenade, sails, tanning oil, Denis Walter
sings carols this night & nights
forever after

       ~ blink ~

    three two one & you're gone

swept off

       into summer's slim pickings

destiny's rotting-fruit horizon

    ~ the bell peals ~

splash & squeal of banquet in the sun

salon—

     It's skin patrol

oily dip scaly fish—Hoist them up they slip

   straight down—

Babies!

Ada's way

'Let's/go out there//& do the poem'
—Michele Leggott

These days we sleepwalk
back & forth
      along the promenade—
same faces, same
prams—
      Yet here
in the garden
          we pause
beneath dogwood's creamy flowers
the copper beech
          & spotted gum
brace sky &
      cloud, for look!
              you're awake
& here we are, together—
blue sage
      by the fountain—
              Yes, we're gazing out
at all the green
      thriving things, paying attention
as best we can—

Aspect

Thirty-five pepper trees encircle
    the park—I counted them
to pass time

    while you slept. The helicopter
rose from the hospital's
    roof. Twice

I counted those trees, wishing it right
    for you. 'Measure
twice, cut once'—

    the maxim, in the years
of hanging plaster. The blade precise
    scoring sheets.

Morning light turning strange—
    smoke sweeping in
from the east.

Scott's shuffle

'Living
        in the world

    is a
        demanding

      &

      scrupulous
business'—

                        'I don't
                    hold
                      a hose, *mate*'—

Seam

Down by the carousel
fishermen are back
in droves. Nights

there's talk of what
comes next. A rainbow
lingers over the city—

the baby waves
to bollards, seagulls
couples sipping coffee

out of paper cups.
The bitter edge to it—
what comes next?

Painted horses stuck
in pose. Fins of dolphin
dark beyond the pier.

Commuter daydream, approaching Little River Station

'Don't be so dramatic about it, Chuck—
    You're saying it's a falsehood…Sean Spicer
        gave alternative facts'
                —Kellyanne Conway

    On the weedy verge
Bugs Bunny is
        singing
            An American Trilogy
in a soiled white
        Presley suit.

A nod to Doctor Williams, on the afternoon pram walk in the Geelong Botanic Gardens

At the edge
of a gravel path
winding amongst
camellias

I found it
purely by chance—
& knew it only
by its sign

SAXIFRAGA—
& not a rock
to split in
sight!

Reading John Berger & Jean Mohr's *A Fortunate Man* in the St Mary's Hall medical library

there's a smell of toast	I hadn't counted on this—	white sky presses
from the cleaner's breakfast	subtle ways of seeing	on stained glass—
for the door is open	leaf after leaf reveal	the urge to step
to step through	itself. Now rain on	into strange seasons
pages— past	timber boards— now	to see deeper
landscape's curtain—	breathe in this space—	than forest's edge. Now
& breathe in in this space—		breathe in this space—

Remedial manoeuvres

Set eyes to sky with luck some days a pie
might fall! Or better still, *kid*
pull the blind & take a look:
    sixteen ibis—
beating thirty-two wings—
veering west & gone
in the dawn.

    *

    Sore neck: 'pinched nerve'. Saw what?
'Bin chickens'. Sun, soar
over pies—
Pines!

    *

    Stretch. Loosen up. *Threskiornis molucca.*
Marks on paper, wings
    to dust. Fly faster?
        MORE WOK

Sublunary gestures at North Arm Cove, in winter

—for David Musgrave

Celebrate stillness as rigour
& delight in motion's
grace—

Brahminy Kite
carves circles in blue fields
of glass—

Summon tides or *tines*, sunlight
flashing on a dolphin's
back—

Let whimsy dance with clouds
in pools amongst
the rocks—

May talk drift to kingfishers
Fernand & the will
to change—

Mix fierce potions in the dusk!
Adie likes a little acid
in her jar—

Currong Street South

    Bob's eyes
  on the wall
      stare you straight
in the eye

      *

    Pink eyes at night—
                Warhol's delight!

     *

      Scenes of Life:
'Camellia hedge monkey-slide tree'. Mountain hides
      in winter sky. Tour or
        map?

      Blue Atlas?

      Blue poles!

          'Stop licking my ear'

Transvaal Square

The child
        doesn't finish her bread
& sausage
     at the rally
for Gaza. She'd rather run
         & play on the grass
& she does.
     She does.

Days

—for RFL

Seven years
   since I read
Williams'
'The Rewaking'
   at Kit's
funeral.
   Spring rekindled—
the sun
   itself revived
by love.
   Thought of it
today
   reading
Rakosi's
'George Oppen,
tbe last
days'—
   elegy
for one who
'upheld
   the integrity
of nouns'.
   We seldom speak

of such
    things—
never mind.
The point—
    if there is one—
I'll let you
decide.
    Let me turn
once more
    to Rakosi:
'Cellist,
        easy on that bow.'

Notes

'Grape days': 'Ten thousand women/and I/ the only one/in boots', *Lorine Niedecker Collected Works* (University of California Press: 2002). The poem also quotes a number of times from Jo Langdon's *Glass Life* (Five Islands Press: 2018), as well as an earlier manuscript version of Langdon's text.

'Sunday radio': 'que Dalila lia', quotation from Max Jacob, sourced from Collin, W. E. (1931). T. S. Eliot. *The Sewanee Review*, 39(1), 17.

'January pastoral': 'Does either Mr Bedient, Mr Hughes or myself know what a hangman thinks?', Veronica Forrest-Thomson, *Poetic artifice: A theory of twentieth-century poetry* (Manchester University Press: 1978).

'Ribbons': includes direct quotation from Brodie, A., Pavey, T., Newton, C., & Sendall, M. C. (2021). Australian bus drivers' modifiable and contextual risk factors for chronic disease: A workplace study. *PloS one*, 16(7), e0255225.

'Correspondence': An elegy for Lee Harwood, the poem makes reference to Harwood's 'The Artful' from *Collected Poems* (Shearsman Books: 2004).

'Suspension': misquotes Barbara Guest's 'Parachutes, my love, could carry us higher', *The Collected Poems of Barbara Guest* (Wesleyan University Press: 2008).

'Ride': 'Coney Island of the mind/to the Coney /Island of the flesh' from 'Clickety-Clack', *The Collected Poems of Paul Blackburn* (Persea Lamplighter: 1984).

'Suns': quote from *The Collected Poems of Larry Eigner* (Stanford University Press: 2010).

'Soloist intimations': Quoted passage—beginning 'But the farmers had moved away' to 'All—except Frederick'—from Leo Lionni's *Frederick* (Collins Picture Lions, 1974).

'Scott's shuffle': Initial quotation from the introduction to *Other: British and Irish Poetry since 1970* (Wesleyan University Press: 1999). The second quotation – for any reader unfamiliar with Australian political discourse – is from former Prime Minister Scott Morrison in response to devastating bushfires in 2019.

'Currong Street South': 'Camellia hedge monkey-slide tree' is sourced from Philip Whalen's *Scenes of Life at the Capital* (Wave Books: 2020).

'Days': quotations from *The Collected Poems of William Carlos Williams: Volume 2* (NDP: 1988); Michael Heller's *Carl Rakosi: Man and Poet* (NPF: 1993); Carl Rakosi's *Ex Cranium, Night* (Black Sparrow Press: 1975).

Acknowledgments

Some of these poems have previously appeared in the following publications: *Australian Book Review*, *Australian Book Review: States of Poetry 2016*, *Australian Poetry Journal*, *Best Australian Poems 2016*, *Cordite Poetry Review*, *ETZ*, *Have Your Chill*, *Homings and Departures: Selected Poems from Contemporary China and Australia* (Recent Work Press: 2021), *Island online*, *Mascara Literary Review*, *No Placebos*, *Otoliths*, *Overland*, *OZ-BURP*, *Red Room Poetry: New Shoots Victoria 2017*, *Westerly*. Thank you to the editors of these publications.

*

Thank you to David Musgrave and the team at Puncher & Wattmann for supporting my work. I'd similarly like to thank Kent MacCarter for his friendship, and encouragement with my writing, over many years. My thanks to Pete Spence—who published many of these poems in his Donnithorne Street Press magazines—and also to Liam Ferney, who generously read the poems in manuscript form. Finally, to my family—Jo and Ada especially—thank you for helping shape the poems in this book, and for your love and encouragement.

www.ingramcontent.com/pod-product-compliance
Lightning Source LLC
Chambersburg PA
CBHW022121090426
42743CB00008B/948